Contents

Contents

CHAPTER 1

A Land of Castles

The medieval world was a military society. It had to be. In around AD 476, the Roman Empire finally fell before concerted barbarian onslaughts, leading to an era of near perpetual violence, invasion and instability. Marauding tribes – Huns, Goths, Vandals – spread terror across great swathes of Europe. This was no brief encounter. Even before the Romans abandoned their imperial province of Britannia in around AD 426, its inhabitants were receiving the destructive attentions of Anglo-Saxons from Germany and Denmark. Raiders were still coming three, four and five centuries later, as the Vikings crossed the North Sea from Scandinavia first to raid along the east coast of England, later to displace the established population and settle their territory.

Wherever they went and whoever they were, the attackers left a trail of disaster and death behind them. They ravaged settlements, villages and towns. They sacked monasteries and churches where tempting treasure could be found. Murder, mayhem and pillage became the currency of the time, and survival was at a premium. Early victims – like the Britons living in Scarborough, which was raided by the Anglo-Saxons in AD 409 – were virtually helpless before this storm of brutal aggression. In time, though, the response that developed was characterised by self-defence of ever-increasing power and ingenuity.

The earliest defences comprised huge earthworks, timber-built forts, sometimes incorporating stonework, or motte and bailey castles. The motte and bailey, the first of which was built on the River Loire in France around AD 990, was a mound, sometimes with a wooden tower, surrounded by a moat and topped by a wooden palisade. This was primitive compared with the more romantic, yet at the same time much more daunting, medieval castle, a vast, complex stone-built structure with walls several feet thick, heavily fortified towers and a drawbridge spanning a deep moat.

This mighty fortress developed in the eleventh and twelfth centuries, but despite its fearsome aspect and the chances it offered for tenacious defence, its purpose was no longer solely military, but political and social as well. Gradually, over time, the nomadic raiders who once lived in the saddle, moving from one scene of pillage and slaughter to the next, settled down into more permanent communities. Now, they lived in towns, villages or hamlets, and became farmers, woodsmen or fishermen.

This did not mean a peaceful or even civilised society. Europe was still a dangerous place, still at the mercy of outlaws, brigands and troublemakers. In this context, the castle acquired a fresh function for the ruling elite, as a means of control over their neighbourhood and its inhabitants. It became a forbidding presence looming over the landscape, and acted as a warning to potential wrongdoers. It was also an unmistakable statement of wealth and power and stood as a sign that the local lord could be disobeyed or challenged only at great personal risk.

The Normans who constructed the first substantial castles in Britain after their invasion of 1066 certainly used them as a deterrent to anyone minded to resist their rule. The punitive nature of the Norman resolve to be absolute masters in their newly conquered territory was demonstrated in the north of England where their response to rebellion in 1069–70 was savage in the extreme. They devastated the region, set fire to crops, killed cattle, burned homes, slaughtered the inhabitants, and smashed the farming implements that might have enabled the survivors to remake some sort of life for themselves.

Fortunately, the depredations in the north of England were not an everyday event. But it came to typify just how far King William was willing to go to assert his authority. The dread lesson sank deep into the English consciousness. Afterwards, even a glimpse of a Norman castle across a field or rising above the horizon or the trees in the forest was a stern reminder of the price disobedience exacted and might exact again.

Ironically, this grim symbol of strength and retribution also suggested a certain weakness in the feudal system by which the Normans and their Plantagenet successors ruled in England. Feudalism was a pyramid arrangement, with the king at its apex. His magnates and the tenants and labourers on their estates occupied the ranks below and each owed fealty and obedience to those who belonged to the rank above. Although this gave the appearance of binding society tightly together through interlocking duties and obligations, the system was essentially decentralised.

Decentralisation was not normally a problem where a king, such as William I, exercised firm control over his realm; but it was a recipe for trouble where a king was too weak, too lazy or too preoccupied elsewhere. This last was the case with several Norman and Plantagenet monarchs who spent a lot of time out of England, in Normandy, Aquitaine, Anjou, Maine or any other of their many possessions in what is now modern France. In this situation, ambitious magnates acquired too much independence to do as they pleased. What they often pleased to do was to use their private armies to attack their neighbours, purloin their lands and their castles and sometimes their entire estates.

In this situation, the features of the classic medieval castle could not afford to derive from architectural fashion or even to reflect the creativity of its designers. Everything about a castle had to serve some purpose of defence for a garrison tasked with fighting off would-be attackers and protecting the magnate and his family and the tenants and workers who fled within its walls for safety in time of war.

For example, the roofs at the top of castle towers were rounded and slanted so as to deflect missiles flung by siege machines. The slits in the walls that served as windows were to protect the archers stationed behind them, while they, by contrast, could fire at enemies with impunity. The drawbridge that spanned the castle moat and comprised the main entrance was hinged at one end to allow it to be drawn up and placed flush against the walls to prevent enemies getting in. This and other gateways could be blocked by a heavy metal grating, the portcullis. Other entrances could be hidden by cunning stonework design and remain unknown to everyone except the castle's inhabitants. Enemies who managed to get past these devices and penetrate the castle would find themselves confronted with steeply winding spiral staircases where the advantage was with the defender: he would be striking downwards with sword or spear at a foe fighting upwards while attempting to climb the stairs and avoid being unbalanced in the process.

The castle as fortress inevitably led to the castle as home. For the members of a noble or royal family, it was the only accommodation that could be regarded as reasonably secure. 'Castle families' were not usually permanent residents but were constantly moving between their scattered manors or estates.

An important reason for frequent moves was the need for a magnate to pay regular visits to his estates, where his feudal duties included settling disputes, hearing petitions, sorting out problems of inheritance following the death of a tenant, even arranging remarriages for widows or at least suggesting suitable candidates. The lord might convene a council in order to take advice from his vassals over important decisions, such as going to war. There were fiefs or grants of land to be made to a new vassal, and the symbolic commendation ceremony to be performed in which the newcomer paid homage to the magnate and swore an oath of fealty to him.

Just as a feudal manor and its adjacent lands formed an essentially self-contained unit, so its castle had to be self-sufficient. Huge supplies of food and water needed to be kept in store, together with plenty of kindling for fires, straw for the stables, rushes for bedding, cooking utensils and a myriad other items that catered for the comfort, sustenance and personal requirements of the magnate's family and retainers.

Despite their peripatetic existence, a noble family found it possible to enjoy a fair standard of luxury, with many refinements not usually featured in the popular view of castle life. The communal sleeping arrangements that obtained before the thirteenth century appear crude, with everyone bedding down on straw palliasses laid out on the floor. But in time the magnate and his lady were able to withdraw to their own room, the solar, where a soft bed covered with fine linen sheets awaited them. This afforded a previously unknown degree of privacy. Advances were also made in the way castles were heated, with fireplaces set into the walls. Sophisticated systems fed water directly into the castle. Some castles even had bathrooms with piped water for washing instead of the tubs that had to be laboriously filled by a team of servants.

Not all castles promised such benefits, of course, but those that did offered a very welcome prospect for a household on the move. However, whether or not comfort lay at the end of the journey, the way there led along rough, potentially dangerous roads and across a landscape where security could never be guaranteed.

CHAPTER 2

On the Road

Travelling from one castle to the next was an expedition rather than a journey. In medieval times, royal and some of the greater noble households took to the roads, on average, about once a month, sometimes even less, and did so in all weathers. This meant that the marshal, the high-ranking, often military, officer who was in charge of organising the journey, had many factors to take into account. Not least was the sheer size of a medieval household on the move. The lord, his lady and their entourage took to the roads in procession, together with hundreds of servants, packhorses and hunting dogs, and an assortment of carriages, carts and wagons loaded with luggage, household goods, cooking utensils and supplies. Kings or important nobles might need as many as twenty wagons and carts to hold everything they needed to take with them, including their treasuries.

A vital component of the journey was an escort of heavily armed and armoured soldiers – anything up to one hundred men – whose task it was to protect the household and particularly the money, jewels and other valuables it carried, against the perils to be found on the open road. This particularly applied to roads that led through, or ran close to, the forests.

Wolves, boars, wild dogs, wild cats and bears, all regarded as predatory beasts in medieval times, proliferated in the forests. So did outlaws, whose image might have been romanticised in medieval tales, but who were, in reality, a constant danger to travellers. It has been reckoned that for every miscreant convicted by the courts, ten others were pronounced outlaws. These criminals and desperadoes, often violent and dangerous, had managed to escape the law, usually by running away, but were sentenced instead to an even worse fate than retributive medieval justice could normally devise.

The outlaw was a non-person who had lost everything that mattered – work, income, food, home, family and freedom – except for the dubious freedom of the forest. Above all, he was denied the protection of the law, and had no feudal liege lord to call his own. In towns or villages, an outlaw was always in danger of being recognised and apprehended. His only hope was to elude his pursuers by reaching sanctuary in a church. Even then, sanctuary was limited and the moment would surely come after a few days, or even hours, when the fugitive was either handed over to the authorities or turned out to face the mob waiting outside.

The long, slow, well-equipped, well-supplied parade of a household with a treasury and other valuables on board was a great temptation to outlaws. Many of them had been pushed so far beyond the bounds of misery and desperation that there was no one, however mighty, however well protected, whom they feared to attack. Outlaw bands were known to haunt several medieval roads and there were even 'black spots', such as stretches of the Great North Road between London and the north of England or parts of the countryside near Aylesbury in Buckinghamshire where ambushes, assaults and robberies were common.

In addition, the roads themselves were a risky proposition. In wet weather, they could become virtual rivers. In freezing temperatures, they iced up and might be almost impassable for wheeled vehicles. There were no signposts, although some roads had milestones. The splendid Roman roads, built a thousand years earlier, had long ago decayed and had never been properly restored. A household journeying between the more far-flung estates of their lord could use major roads – London to Exeter, London to Bristol – but even in the best conditions, the way could be uncomfortable as well as protracted.

Except for the towns, most medieval roads were unsurfaced and unpaved. Rural roads were often little more than well-worn tracks with big grass verges on either side. Some, at least, were reasonably wide, since they had to cope with the mass movement of troops or large herds of sheep and cattle. A decree of King Henry I, issued in 1118, established that the 'royal way' must be wide enough to allow two wagons to pass each other or sixteen mounted knights to ride abreast.

A travelling household, however, had to confront whatever conditions prevailed on the road as it wound and jolted its way through the countryside, stretched out for perhaps hundreds of yards, far from centres of habitation and succour for a large part of the way. In these circumstances, a household had to be self-sufficient. Enough food, drink and fuel for cooking needed to be carried, with a good supply of blankets for colder weather or protection against sudden storms. Chairs or ground-coverings, such as carpets, were required to allow the riders to dismount and relax or relieve any saddle-sores they had suffered on the road. All supplies and utensils had to be unpacked, laid out, packed again and stored away before the household could set off once more.

Although these breaks in a long and arduous journey were very necessary, they naturally increased travelling time. It has been reckoned that in medieval England, it was possible to cover about 20 or 30 miles in a day. But that was on horseback, whereas large numbers of people in a household on the move made their way on foot. Carts and wagons bumping over the unmade roads slowed the procession down even further and more halts had to be made to rest the horses.

All this made for a very long, very tiring day for all concerned and had an important influence on the logistics of the journey. Starting out at, or soon after, dawn was imperative if optimum use were to be made of daylight, especially in winter. Even then, many journeys could not be completed in a single day. The marshal of the household had to organise overnight halts – sometimes as many as three during a single journey – either at a monastery, the more respectable and comfortable choice, or, if none were located along the route, at an inn or tavern.

Although inns as such were not a new innovation in medieval times (they were popular as far back as the days of ancient Rome) they did not arise in any great number in England until the twelfth and thirteenth centuries. The catalyst, it appears, came about after 1170, when Thomas Becket, King Henry II's Archbishop of Canterbury, was murdered in the town's cathedral. With this, Canterbury became the focus for pilgrims visiting Becket's shrine. They arrived in such great numbers that inns were set up along the route to cater for them. The inns, which provided lodgings and substantial feasts if required, must have been a cheery sight for weary travellers, with their bright, warm welcome at the end of a hard day on the road.

The tavern was a more lively, even riotous, alternative to the inn, the ancestor of the English pub, offering plenty of wine to drink – apparently the only drink they sold. Customers could gamble, enjoy music and singing or procure prostitutes as part of the entertainment. It was also possible to buy wine there to take away. Branches and leaves were hung over the door as a sign that this was for sale. Food could also be purchased, although this was frequently obtained from an independent cook shop nearby and consumed in the tavern.

Next morning, the itinerant household moved on, perhaps spending another night at the next inn or tavern along the way. As they approached their destination, it was time to alert staff at the castle to their imminent arrival. While the lord and his household were elsewhere, the castle was relatively quiet and life could be leisurely. Domestic staff and even the garrison might be reduced, unless there was a particular danger in the area that meant a castle needed a comprehensive defence. By contrast, the imminent arrival of the lord, lady and their household was a clarion wake-up call.

The first sign of their approach comprised a party of outriders galloping on ahead to make sure that all was ready to receive them. For security against an enemy attempting to trick the guards into opening the gate, an outrider would carry a spear from which the lord's personal standard fluttered, so that the guards, recognising it, would grant entry to the advance party.

There are records from the early twelfth century indicating that two bakers rode with the outriders, ready to prepare and bake bread in the castle kitchen, so that it would be ready to eat by the time the household arrived. The bakers were not alone. The castle cooks got to work in the kitchens, putting finishing touches to the mass of food the household was going to require. Meanwhile, out in the courtyard, grooms stood by to stable the hundreds of horses that were soon to arrive. The castle servants made ready to help with unpacking the carts and wagons the household had brought with them.

As the lord of the castle rode in, he received the obeisances due to him. The rest of the household followed, rolling in across the castle drawbridge until they were all inside and it could be drawn up tight against the outside wall. The expedition was over, at least until the time came to move on once again.

CHAPTER 3

A Day in the Life of a Feudal Lord

A medieval castle was essentially a communal environment. The hub of activity, by day and by night, was the great hall where the lord and lady, their officials and advisers, and most of their household ate, worked, socialised and kept their dogs, hunting falcons and other pets. It was here that the business of the estate took place and that tenants with rent to pay, petitions to be presented or problems to be laid before their lord for judgement queued up for their share of his attention.

Even sleeping at night was a communal business. The great hall was like a vast bedroom, in which only the lord and lady had a degree of privacy: they slept naked in a bed on a raised dais at the back of the hall, with a curtain to separate them from the rest of the household. By the thirteenth century, this separation had evolved into a small private chamber or a recess in the wall.

Some castle halls had more than one storey, in which case separate bedrooms were available behind the gallery, but only for the lord's family and favoured officials. Less important members of the household slept, in varying degrees of discomfort, on benches lining the walls of the great hall. Others lay wherever they could find space on the floor, which was usually made of beaten earth, stone or plaster. Straw palliasses were spread out as mattresses, with rugs or cloaks for 'bedclothes'.

The great hall was likely to be warm at night. During the eleventh and twelfth centuries, an open fire burned in the centre of the room. This later evolved into a safer method of heating – fireplaces recessed into the walls. Unfortunately, proper chimneys were rarely, if ever, provided. The only escape for the smoke was a crude flue which often swirled it about the hall aided by constant draughts. Only when tapestries were hung on the walls, a fashion that became popular in the fourteenth and fifteenth centuries, did draughts come under some control.

In addition to the choked atmosphere, the floor could be a rather unpleasant place to sleep. Carpets were unknown in castles until around the thirteenth century and even then they were usually reserved to the separate room or 'solar' occupied by the lord and lady. Everyone else had to make do with a floor covering of rushes or straw, which was scattered about with herbs – and for a very good reason. Everything that fell on the floor in the great hall – bits of food, bones, splashes of oil, spilled wine or beer as well as the droppings of dogs, cats, monkeys, birds and other pets and miscellaneous dirt – might be left there to moulder and rot and so create some very unpleasant smells.

The day's activity began early, soon after dawn. First order of business for the lord was to put on the drawers that served as his underwear. The lady did likewise, donning a long chemise. Then, both washed their faces in a basin of cold water and dressed in the rest of their clothes which were essentially the same for both – two tunics, a mantle, fur-lined in winter, belts secured by gold, silver or jewelled clasps at the waist, and the long hose and slippers that served for indoor wear. In the twelfth century, ladies wore a simple white veil or later, in the thirteenth, a wimple secured by a stiff cap. Lofty jewelled headdresses for women or fur collars and cuffs and long pointed leather shoes for men did not appear until the fifteenth century.

Once dressed, the lord and lady made their way to the castle chapel, where they joined the rest of their household as the chaplain, or chancellor, said Mass. Next came the first meal of the day, a rather modest affair for most people, comprising a pot of ale and a large piece of bread. The lord himself might have something more elaborate, such as white bread, cold meat or a glass of wine. After that, he repaired to the great hall to attend to the business of the day.

Feudal lords earned most of their headlines in history by their better known activities such as making war, usually with each other, taking part in tournaments, or tussling for a share of power with autocratic kings such as John, Henry III or, much later, Richard II. These, though, were not a lord's major concerns. What occupied most of his time and thought was his estates and land, their productivity, day-to-day running and security. Without these things, a feudal lord's influence, his status and his wealth were non-existent. In this context, the feudal castle was the guardian of a lord's lands against all comers, as well as the visible sign of his power.

The morning session began with meetings between the lord of the castle and his senior officials, the constable who was in charge of security, the marshal who was overseer of the 'outside staff' such as stable grooms or huntsmen, the chamberlain whose duties included caring for the household valuables, and the seneschal or bailiff, who took care of the castle accounts. The seneschal was required to keep meticulous records in order to give the lord a clear picture of the state of his castle and estates. From these records, the lord learned how much food had been produced on his lands, how much timber had been felled, what services had been discharged or taxes paid, even how many acres in each of the estate's fields had been sown with wheat, rye, barley, oats, peas, beans and other crops.

While in residence at his castle, a feudal liege lord had to wear many 'hats'. He was the protector of his vassals and tenants, he acted as arbiter of any disputes that might arise, he was the judge where matters of law were involved, the legal guardian of underage heirs to tenants' landholdings, and he even played matchmaker, choosing a new husband for a widow.

By ten or eleven o'clock in the morning, the administrative business had usually been concluded and it was time for the main meal of the day. The variety was enormous, with all manner of meat, game and fowl, together with a great amount of fruit and vegetables, cheese, butter and bread. A salad could consist of parsley, garlic, leeks, sage, fennel, mint, rosemary and rue with a dressing of salt, vinegar and oil or crab apple juice. Food was eaten with the fingers, while inedible items, such as bones, were thrown to the pet dogs that circled the tables in search of titbits. The lord, his lady and the high officials drank wine, the lesser functionaries of the household, ale or cider. When the meal was over, the chaplain's almoner gathered up all the scraps and remaining bones, pieces of bread soaked in stew or soup and other leftovers and delivered them to the poor of the district as the lord of the castle's gift of alms.

After the meal the lord was usually free to enjoy his favourite afternoon activities – hunting or hawking. When hawking was in prospect, the lord kept his falcon sitting on the back of his chair throughout the main meal. If, by any chance, was free from his feudal duties, he delighted in a day's hawking or hunting, sometimes spending the entire time in the forest revelling in the chase.

It could be a hot, dusty, sweaty day and the bath that awaited the lord's return was very welcome. A wooden tub was set up and a stool placed inside for the lord to sit on. Servants scrubbed him with soap made from soda, wood ash and meat fat or one of the more luxurious soaps imported from southern Europe which were made from olive oil scented with herbs. Afterwards, the lord might be shaved with a special sharp-edged knife, usually made of bronze. A light supper with family and retainers followed, and as night fell, candles made from wax or rendered animal fat were lit, together with resinous wood torches and rushlights soaked in grease. Those attempting to navigate staircases or dark, draughty corridors did so with the help of a portable lantern in which thin slices of horn shielded the lighted candle inside.

The illumination was modest, though, and pools of darkness remained in the great hall. In addition, the day's work and play at the castle or in the nearby forest could be long and arduous. All of which made it likely that the evening would end early. Once guards and sentries had been posted round the castle, and the grounds around it, cloaked in shadow, had been checked for intruders, all that remained for the lord and lady was to retire to their private room.

The servants had been busy, making sure the fire was lit and the room warm, the bed, with its feather mattress, was properly made and the heavy blankets or fur coverings were clean and neatly spread. The chamberlain, acting as the lord's personal attendant, helped him undress, put away his clothes, provided him with toilet facilities for the night, and placed his nightcap on his head. Then his hair was combed neatly around the cap. Meanwhile, his lady was prepared for bed by her own attendants. Any dogs or other pets were removed from the room, and, at last, after saying their prayers, the couple were able to settle down for the night. Their personal servants curled up nearby to sleep on the floor, wrapped in cloaks or blankets, and as close as possible to the warmth of the fire.

CHAPTER 4

Food and Drink

Food and drink were much more than sustenance in medieval times, and entertaining the household and guests to the main meal of the day more than run-of-the-mill hospitality. The quantity, quality, variety and sheer excess that marked communal eating in the great hall of a castle were designed to indicate a host's wealth and status and advertise the fact that conspicuous consumption and even waste was well within the scope of his purse. Even an ordinary meal, without special guests to impress, was a formidable proposition. The seemingly modest two or three courses provided at these lesser meals were deceptive, for each of them involved numerous dishes: the last, for example, comprised cheese, nuts, fruits, wafers and spiced wine.

Providing anything less than blatant plenty was clearly not an option, but preparing vast meals was a daunting proposition in which scores of people could be involved. The preservation of food was of particular importance, since so much of it was needed at one time and there was always the danger that it might go off, particularly in summer. Salting, smoking and curing in brine were all used to keep meat edible for as long as possible. Another method was to slaughter the animals needed for a meal just before cooking commenced. There were two ways of salting meat, one by dry-salting, which meant covering the meat with salt that had been turned into powder with a mortar and pestle. The second method, curing by brine, involved immersing meat in a strong salt solution. The salt had to be removed before cooking, and this was done by means of repeated soaking and rinsing in clear water.

A vast variety of meat was provided. The menu might include plover, goose, duck, pheasant, thrushes, finches, seagulls, cormorants, venison, peacock, swans, cranes and even vultures. Some of the cooking was done outdoors, as a precaution against fire, but entire animals – pigs, cattle, sheep, poultry or game – were roasted on spits in the castle kitchens. Big iron cauldrons were hung over a fire to cook soups and stews or to boil meat. Some meat went to make rich and elaborate speciality dishes. One of them was *blankmanger*, for which chicken was pounded to a paste, mixed with rice, boiled in almond milk and seasoned with sugar. Once the milk had thickened, the dish was covered in fried almonds and aniseed. As this recipe indicates, sweet and savoury could go together in medieval cooking, perhaps to disguise rancid meat or fish or just because the medieval palate was fond of rich pungent tastes.

Fish was usually served with highly flavoured sauces. Herring, for example, was cooked with ginger, pepper and cinnamon. The castle gardens provided herbs for other sauces, which were made by grinding them to a paste and mixing them with vinegar, mustard, onions, saffron, cloves or wine.

The variety of fish available for the medieval table could be extraordinary. There was mullet, sole, flounder, plaice, ray, mackerel, trout, salmon, pike, crab, crayfish, oysters, eels and shad, a river fish similar to herring. Some of these fish could be taken from the castle's private pond or a stretch of a local river that ran through the estate.

Vegetables such as peas, beans or onions were grown in the castle gardens. The orchard provided apples, pears, plums, peaches and nuts, and the bees kept in the castle apiary or elsewhere on the estate furnished the honey that was used for sweetening. The more exotic fruits, such as dates, raisins, figs, oranges and pomegranates, were usually imports purchased locally, either in a nearby town or at fairs.

Correct procedures were important in virtually every aspect of a meal. After the trestle tables were set up in the great hall and the cloths were spread over them, steel knives, silver spoons and cups, dishes for salt, and the shallow, silver-rimmed wooden bowls known as mazers had to be laid out in exact order. There was also a right way to cut a trencher, a thick slice of bread that served as a 'plate' for eating meat: trenchers were specially hardened by baking and subsequent exposure to the air for a day or two and their purpose was to absorb the vast amount of grease involved in medieval meat dishes. Although eating the 'plate', as it were, was allowed, it was considered better 'form' to leave the trencher as one of the leftovers for distribution to the poor. The poor, in fact, were often present at a meal, for beggars wandered in and out of the great hall, picking up whatever scraps they could find.

Rules also applied to the carving of meat, which was performed by the lord of the castle, and to the number of fingers a servant should use to hold the meat while he did so. There was a set order in which dishes should be served and where they should be placed on the table. When all was ready, horns were blown to alert members of the household and guests that the time had come for them to wash their hands before eating. When they arrived in the great hall, servants were waiting for them with basins of water and towels.

Although knives were provided at table, forks were not commonly used in England until the eighteenth century. Solid food, such as meat, was cut up and eaten with the fingers – or 'God's forks' as they were often called. Table manners were strictly laid down and featured prominently in medieval books of etiquette. No elbows on the table, no belching or burping, no overfilling the mouth, no dipping pieces of meat in the salt dish, no drinking without first wiping the mouth. Order of precedence at table was strictly followed. The high table was reserved for the lord of the castle, his lady and their most important guests, who included a churchman to say Grace. Everyone else attending the meal sat noticeably lower to indicate their lesser status. The high table was also the only place in the great hall where people had the privilege of a plate to themselves. The rest shared a dish and of these, the more important was 'served' by his lowlier companion. Breaking bread at the start of the meal or passing the cup of wine or ale was the task of a younger on behalf of an older man, and a lower-ranked knight for a more senior one. Although the status of women was not particularly high in medieval times, a man did the same for his female 'partner'.

A variety of entertainment was provided for the household and guests both during and after meals. Jugglers and tumblers performed, so did female acrobats and wrestlers. Jesters told jokes and entertained with stories. Troubadours recited love poems. A band of strolling minstrels came into the minstrel's gallery, if there was one, or else took their places at one end of the great hall. They played lutes, harps, gitterns or guitars, rebecs, flutes, pipes, horns, clarions or high-pitched trumpets, bagpipes or the vielle, a stringed instrument similar to the modern viola and played with a bow. One of the guests might do a solo act and sing to entertain his companions while the minstrels provided an accompaniment.

Once the meal was over, the tables were cleared and the bowls of water came out again for people to wash their hands. For those with time to relax, several more entertainments were on offer. The more energetic, taking their sport outside, could bait bears, watch performing bears, or snare falcons for training and future use in hawking. Others, preferring more leisurely recreation indoors, might spend the afternoon performing 'caroles', a dance in which men and women joined hands and sang as they moved round in a circle. Hot cockles, a popular indoor game, involved one player putting on a blindfold, then kneeling down while he was struck by other players whom he had to identify. Backgammon and chess were also played, and so were dice games and a form of billiards.

Card games, imported from the Muslim lands across the Mediterranean Sea, were added to castle entertainment during the thirteenth and fourteenth centuries. At first, card playing was only for the rich, since the packs were hand-painted and extremely expensive. However, card games became more wide-spread with the introduction of wood block printing, which arrived in Europe some time before 1370 and permitted mass production. The cards numbered fifty-two to a pack, were divided into four suits and included picture or court cards, a system brought from Mameluke-ruled Egypt by merchants and travellers and still in use in Europe today.

CHAPTER 5

The Women of the Castle

A castle was essentially a masculine environment. Women were present, but only in small numbers, and usually comprised the lady, her attendants, her personal servants and other functionaries such as laundresses. On the face of it, this, together with the creature comforts of a castle – heating, water supply, drainage and waste disposal systems – might suggest home and family.

But the face of it was deceptive: the outward appearance of a castle was, and was meant to be, daunting, its aspect stern and stony, and it bristled with the armaments and fortifications that betrayed what it really was – a place that might masquerade as a home, but was always ready for the chief business of medieval men: assault and battle.

Sentries stood on guard at vital points, a resident constable or 'castellan' commanded the garrison and was responsible for castle security. The lowlier members of the household, such as grooms, cooks, gardeners and servants, had to be ready, whenever necessary, to do their feudal duty and take up arms to defend the castle and its inhabitants. More advent-urous women might participate in some of its riskier activities, like hawking and hunting, and some were owners of castles in their own right; but the business of a castle predominantly belonged to the men.

This is not to say that the lady of the castle was a totally background character. She could not afford to be, given the circumstances that governed married life for a woman of high rank. At any time, she could be obliged to stand in for her husband when he was called away to war, either at the king's command, on Crusade to the Holy Land or to defend some part of his own, often widely scattered, estates.

Meanwhile, at home, his wife had to protect the family's interests, oversee the running of her husband's lands, direct the castle staff, keep an eye on the family finances and even make legal decisions. Women were also encouraged to familiarise themselves with the multifarious tasks of the seneschal or steward. This role could be so onerous and wide ranging that by the thirteenth century, large estates had not one seneschal but two, one to handle estate business, the other to take care of victualling the household.

Paradoxically, the women who were expected to take on such responsibilities and hand the family estates back to their husbands in good order were accorded a very lowly status in law. Legally, they were chattels, 'owned' by their fathers before marriage and by their husbands after it. Once wed, a wife came 'under the rod' or 'control' of her husband. He could do anything he liked with her property, even sell it against her wishes, and she had no right to gainsay him. She could not appear in court unless he accompanied her, and she needed his consent if she wanted to make a will. A wife was also expected to make herself 'pleasing' to him, adorning herself with perfume and, despite the opposition of the Church to such frippery, reddening her lips and cheeks with ochre or whitening her skin with flour to make it appear more delicate and hide imperfections.

However, not all wives were the doormats and cyphers these rules implied. There are records of pugnacious, outspoken women, but more often than not, these were women whose great self-confidence and unrestrained vocabulary derived from their status as daughters of powerful titled families. One such was Isabella, Countess of Arundel who, in 1252, publicly berated King Henry III for claiming the wardship of an orphan whose care rightfully belonged to her. After accusing the King of dishonest practice, Isabella went on: 'When, my lord, do you avert your face from justice? . . . You do not govern well, either yourself or us.' She then swept out of the King's presence without asking the usual permission, leaving him standing speechless.

Of course, most women, who were literally or metaphorically 'under the rod', lacked the opportunity, character or nerve to emulate the bellicose Countess of Arundel. For them, it was only when they were widowed that they had the chance to gain some measure of personal freedom. A widow had the right in law to inherit one-third of her husband's estates. She could plead in court on her own behalf for the return of the personal property she had brought to the marriage, even if her late husband had sold it in the meantime. For as long as she remained unwed, a widow could exercise the rights given to freemen, those men who were not the property of a feudal lord, which included the right to earn money and to own land.

It is hardly surprising, then, that with such unaccustomed liberties on offer for the first time in their lives, many widows refused to remarry. One such was Isabella Forz, Countess of Devon and Aumale, who married at the age of 13 and had five children before her husband William died in 1261, when she was 25. She lived another thirty-two years, but remained a widow throughout. Instead, the Countess became owner of Carisbrooke Castle on the Isle of Wight and a major landowner with an income of £2,500 a year – a vast fortune for the time.

The early widowhood of Isabella Forz was by no means unusual in medieval times, and resulted, inevitably, from the realities of contemporary life. Marriages were often arranged between families of similar social standing. Wives, or rather potential wives, could be betrothed as early as the age of 5 and married seven or eight years later. Husbands, however, were usually older than their brides, sometimes much older. Among the nobility, men rarely married before they were of age, or were the owners of land. Husbands, therefore, were rather more likely to die first. There was another factor. Many young men were killed in the ongoing wars of the Middle Ages, or died from injuries suffered on the battlefield. In these circumstances, widows as young as 17 or 18 years of age were not unknown.

Their very different destinies in medieval society were reflected in the education given to boys and girls. Both were sent away to other households to be educated, for it was thought that parents would pamper their own children, but be stricter and more impartial with someone else's. Given the number of infections and diseases that then prevailed, life in the Middle Ages could be both dangerous and short, and physicians were frequently unable to diagnose what was wrong, let alone cure it. It was therefore important for children to mature quickly, and sending them to grow up in other households assisted in this process. There, both boys and girls could mix with people of their own age and class. Under this regime, it was hoped that they would mature fast.

The boys were mainly educated for battle, training in horsemanship and the use of weapons or jousting at tournaments, which were the rehearsals for war. Some boys were literate, but reading and writing were not universally regarded as manly virtues: such activities were more often seen as fit only for clerks, priests and women. Girls, on the other hand, were educated to read, write and speak courtly French and Latin, the latter, in its medieval form, the lingua franca of Europe. Their education included domestic skills: girls learned how to weave cloth, embroider, play musical instruments and sing songs. A girl was also taught the social conventions – gracious manners, polite conversation, how to address dignitaries – in preparation for her future as lady of a castle, receiving and welcoming visitors in appropriate style. Music, song and embroidery, together with setting and solving riddles, were regular pastimes for ladies of the castle and their attendants, as was reading poetry – and, for those women who were suitably gifted, writing it as well.

Medieval poetry could be lavishly lyrical and expressed an adoration of women that was totally at odds with the reality of their position in society. Here, in an emotionally heightened world all its own, poetry idealised women as the focus of courtly love. In the stories, songs and poems purveyed by troubadours, the poet–minstrels who entertained at royal or noble courts and castles, a lady's lover was dazzled by her grace and beauty and accorded her all the elaborate courtesies known to chivalry. Husbands were excluded because this artificial, stylised relationship drew its glamour from the fact that it was illicit.

Whether fictional or real, courtly love required a suitor to lavish gifts and tokens on his lady, together with songs, poems, bouquets, elaborate gestures of devotion and many lovelorn sighs. Courtly love was essentially a game, part fantasy, part daydream, part theatre, and one that had to be played from afar. It was safer that way, for if courtly love were to turn physical, the ensuing adultery could damage the husband's honour and incite revenge. An errant lady of the castle could be banished, imprisoned or placed in a nunnery for life. Her lover might be mutilated and killed.

This encouraged courtly love to retain its chastity. As such, it was able to evolve in time into a new form of fiction – romantic literature – which in its purest form still reflects the same medieval virtues.

CHAPTER 6

The Children of the Castle

The pressures of the Middle Ages allowed no time or inclination for the modern concept of child-hood as a magical period of sheltered innocence. Rather, childhood was seen as an inconvenience that got in the way of serious living and the feudal role that all nobles, male and female, needed to assume. This was exemplified by the way young girls and boys were dressed: there was no such thing as children's clothes, only downsized versions of adult fashions that made them look like miniature grown-ups. Adults and children even enjoyed some of the same pastimes – 'hoodman blind', one of the many variations on blind man's buff, playing with dice, fivestones, skipping with ropes or whipping tops. On one occasion in 1152, King Stephen, no less, was discovered playing 'knights', a game similar to 'conkers', with a 5-year-old boy.

Sending sons and daughters away from home at around the age of 7 to be brought up by other noble families was not the first family separation that children experienced. Soon after birth, they were given over to wet-nurses to be fed and nurtured through the first few months and years of their lives. Just as childbirth was a perilous enterprise for mothers, who all too often died in the process, so the survival of their infants was always uncertain. Even royal and noble infants, who presumably lived in the best environments, could fall foul of the dangers of their time, which included runaway infections and epidemics, breech births, untreatable birth defects, or insanitary conditions. The process of birth was itself unpredictable and there was a special prayer of thanksgiving for mothers who survived the ordeal. All the same, the incidence of stillbirths or deaths in infancy or early childhood was always high. For every ten children born in the Middle Ages, between three and five were likely to die in infancy, and of the survivors, two or three would die in their teens or sooner. The average life expectancy was no more than 25 or 30.

All this afforded plenty of reason for medieval society to hurry children into adulthood. But there were also social, financial and, for the boys, military purposes to be served. The obvious reason for girls to be married at the age of 13 or 14 was to take as much advantage as possible of their childbearing years, which could well be curtailed by death in pregnancy or childbirth. The incidence of death in infancy or early childhood made it necessary to have as large a family as possible and as quickly as possible, to counter this tragic wastage.

Another, more cynical, reason for marrying daughters at an early age was to avoid depredations of the family estate by the king or other magnates. The guardianship of a young girl whose parents died before she was old enough to be married could be a tempting source of influence and income. A legal guardian, once his position was official, had almost complete power over his ward. He could sell or confiscate her property, and even sell the guardianship, for a fee, to another magnate anxious to profit from what was a very lucrative business. Kings, always seeking private sources of income, were particularly predatory and difficult to gainsay once they set their sights on a lucrative guardianship. Parents anxious to preserve their family estates saw in a husband who gained control of his young wife and all her possessions a means of short-circuiting these practices.

Marriage for love was not unknown in medieval times, but marriage by arrangement was much more common. The marriage of convenience, in which parents were the prime movers, was an accepted part of a package that allowed young people of noble families to marry within their class. This preserved family honour and made sure that any future children would have the best chance to continue the aristocratic line.

Sending girls to be brought up by other noble families was the preliminary part of the package. These girls grew up and were trained and educated along with other young people from similar backgrounds so that their social group was forged very early on and the temp-tation to stray outside it was curtailed.

A castle could therefore house a number of boys and girls from different noble families in what might be termed a co-educational boarding school. The presence of numerous boys was especially important because the training of young males, like so much else about castle life, was a communal affair. The castle served as a mil-itary training ground for boys, first as squires in attend-ance on knights, then as knights in their own right.

It could take several years to turn a young boy into a competent squire and several more years for him to become eligible to join an order of chivalry as a fully fledged knight. The whole procedure was designed to be a course in humility and service, from grooming horses in the stables, to learning how to wait on his lord at table and present him with his wine-cup on bended knee. Etiquette demanded that a squire in training must not sit down until told to, and he was warned against several solecisms – scratching himself, leaning on the table, making a mess on the cloth, drinking with a full mouth. Nose-, teeth- and nail-picking were also considered the height of bad manners. Some trainee squires took turns to attend the lord of the castle in the morning, helping him to dress, combing his hair or selecting the clothes he was to wear.

By the time he was 14, a boy was expected to be a practised fencer and hunter, skilled at hawking, horsemanship and at fighting in the lists. Medieval castles had their own lists, also known as tiltyards, sited above the moat between the chief curtain wall and the outer battlements. For the squires, this was an important training ground. Tourneys and tournaments might have been regarded as sports, but they were, in reality, rehearsals for war. In the tiltyard, squires learned precision in the use of weapons at the quintain, a wooden dummy hung from a post. The quintain spun rapidly as they approached it, riding their horses at high speed, lance grasped in the hand. The trick was to strike the quintain with the lance and ride on before the dummy could spin round again and strike a blow of its own. It took time and effort for squires to learn the art of tilting and getting out of the way of a counterstrike, which in real battle against a real opponent could mean serious injury or death. Often, in training, the quintain unhorsed the squire, who sprawled on the ground to ribald comments from his companions and the fury of his tutor.

The tiltyard was certainly the school of hard knocks, but the training did not end there. Squires needed to train for fighting in real battle while wearing full armour. At the same time, they had to be lithe and nimble despite the weight of steel that encased them from head to toe. To this end, they were required to leap into the saddle without touching the stirrup, and roll over on the ground and leap up in one movement to confront an enemy – all while wearing full armour.

The culmination of all the hard work, gruelling practice, bumps, scrapes and other injuries sustained in training was the ceremony in which, with great solemnity, a squire became a knight. The night before the dubbing ritual took place, the young man kept vigil in the castle chapel until dawn. He washed himself, symbolising spiritual as well as bodily cleanliness. When dawn broke, he celebrated Mass. Next, he dressed in a new set of clothes, which, from his underwear to his tunic and ermine cloak, were all white and had been specially made for the occasion to stress his purity and devotion to the knightly ideal. After breakfasting with friends and family, the young man walked out into the open air where his father and several other knights, and sometimes his father's lord, awaited him in the castle courtyard. Together, they helped him put on his armour while minstrels played music and a flourish of trumpets sounded. The young man's sword, which had been blessed the night before by a priest, was brought out to him. He kissed the hilt as a sign of devotion to the holy relics placed inside its pommel. Then, standing before his sponsor, usually his father, he was given the *collé* or buffet. This was meant to be the last blow he would have to suffer without responding in kind. The *collé* could be anything from a gentle tap to a hefty whack with the fist or open hand, so powerful that it could knock the young man off his feet.

Afterwards, he took the knight's oath, and his horse, fully caparisoned and harnessed, was led out. Once he was in the saddle, the new knight's lance and shield were handed to him. And so, in a few hours, the young man passed from youth to manhood and from lowly squire to a new place in an exalted elite.

CHAPTER 7

Servants

In smaller noble households, where a minor lord had less extensive estates, a single steward was able to handle both 'outdoor' and 'indoor' matters, respectively the management of his lord's estates and the domestic arrangements. However, from the thirteenth century onwards, the feudal structure of English medieval society began to change as nobles acquired larger, more widely dispersed estates and, with that, more populous households.

This often came about through wealthy marriages, so that 'super-estates' were formed from lands that heiress wives brought to their new husbands. Naturally, as the size and extent of noble estates increased, the responsibilities of the steward grew and it became common for 'outdoor' and 'indoor' duties to be separated, with a different steward in command of each section.

The Fleta, a late thirteenth-century treatise on English common law, detailed the duties of an 'indoor' steward:

It is the steward's duty to account every night . . . for the expenses of the household, and to ascertain the total of the day's expenditure. It is his duty also to take delivery of flesh and fish of every kind, and this he shall have cut up in his presence and counted as they are delivered to the cook. It is also his business to know precisely how many loaves can be made from a quarter of wheat. Further, he should know how many loaves and portions are appropriate for the household in ordinary (as opposed to guest) days.

The duties of the 'outdoor' steward, usually known as the seneschal, were even more onerous and required specialised knowledge. A seneschal must be acquainted with the law of the realm, keep track of rents and services owed to his lord by the various manors on his estates, keep strict records of the franchises of lands, woods, meadows, pastures, waters, mills and all other features belonging to the manors. The seneschal was, in addition, charged with policing his lord's estates and noting any crimes that had occurred there. This in-cluded trespassing on the lord's parkland, or stealing from ponds, warrens, rabbit runs and dove-houses. Anything and everything that had been unlawfully removed, with subsequent loss to the lord of the estate, had to be reported and, where possible, appropriate action taken.

Highly specialised tasks were performed by some other high-ranking servants of the castle, such as the household chamberlain and the chancellor or chap-lain. The chamberlain was effectively the personal servant of his lord, providing him with bathing facil-ities and taking care of his wardrobe. The chancellor, though classed as a servant, was in fact a great deal more. He was in charge of the castle chapel and the acts of worship performed there, but also fulfilled an extra function in the administration of the household.

Before the thirteenth century, churchmen of various ranks were almost the only literates in medieval society. Consequently, reading, writing, composing letters, keeping archives and giving legal advice to kings and lords were all part of their work. But though at first considered lowly by men who saw their own business – making war – as much more manly, literacy and learning acquired increasing importance. By the thirteenth century, nobles whose predecessors had been content to sign documents with a cross and issue decrees they were unable to read, were starting to become literate themselves.

The churchmen–clerks nevertheless retained their monopoly and larger medieval households employed teams of clerks to handle secretarial and administrative business. The importance of this work was officially recognised in the mid-thirteenth century, when estate management became a regular course taught to young men in search of careers in the service of one of the great lords of England. The course lasted between six months and a year, after which students were able to enter a lord's employ as apprentices. It was a career worth pursuing, for the rewards could be great.

Naturally enough, the tasks that fell to the great mass of castle servants were not so prestigious nor so lucrative as they were for those further up the household hierarchy, but these lesser servants were very well treated and even privileged in some ways Board, lodging and clothes were provided for them, and so were periods of leave to enable them to visit their families. This was particularly welcome to married men among the servants, who had to leave their wives and children behind when they entered their lord's service. The one, quite reasonable, condition normally made was that too many servants should not be away on holiday at the same time.

Rates of pay were modest, though. The humblest members of the staff were lucky to be paid a penny a day. This matched the rate given to the lowliest workers in a royal household, but noble households frequently paid less. One penny in the thirteenth century was the equivalent of £1.96 today. By contrast, a skilled craftsman earned the equivalent of nearly £9 a day and a chancellor, five shillings or close on £118 a day.

The menial work in the household was, of course, extremely labour-intensive. There was a greater awareness of hygiene in medieval society and much more washing, cleaning, sweeping and scrubbing than subsequent ages have presumed. There were fires to be laid and lit, cooking and other utensils to be washed. Vast floors had to be cleaned and scullions laboured long and hard to clear up the mess of oil, fat, hair, blood and gore that had to be removed after animals were cooked on spits.

The number of servants employed in castles with even fair-sized households could be considerable. This applied in particular to staff whose work involved the preparation, cooking and serving of food. The castle larder, pantry and kitchen employed entire staffs of their own, many of them specialists, as were the servants who worked in the buttery, a part of the castle cellar where beverages, particularly ale, were stored. The cellar, where huge butts of beer were kept, was controlled by the castle butler.

There were cupbearers, bakers, brewers, a servant who handled the fruit, another who made wafers, yet another whose task was making candles. Slaughterers killed animals for meat. Poulterers specialised in providing chickens and other fowl for the lord's table. One of the cooks was employed to make sauces. One servant had charge of the tablecloths.

Beyond the kitchens, in the inner ward of the castle, craftsmen and artisans were noisily at work. The castle had to be self-sufficient in many ways, because of its often remote location and the cost and dangers of transporting goods from towns or villages in the area. The castle cobblers made shoes, the armourers fashioned chain mail armour, billers forged axes, coopers made barrels and casks, blacksmiths fashioned ironwork and swords.

Elsewhere, tailors were tasked by the keeper of the wardrobe to make clothes for the lord and livery for his retainers. They required special skills, including an understanding of the latest fashions and expertise in the handling of expensive materials. Their task included making miniature liveries for little boys as young as 7 years old who worked as pages in the castle. A page's duties included waiting at table, helping to care for the lord's clothes and assisting him in getting dressed. Pages also worked as assistants to the squires.

Women were employed as laundresses to wash clothes, tablecloths, sheets and towels, while one churchman, Bogo de Clare, put his laundress to work washing his hair. However, in noble castles, female servants were vastly outnumbered by men and most of the women were employed to attend the lady of the castle, to help her wash and dress, do her hair, care for her wardrobe, pass the time playing games with her and generally keep her company. The most eminent ladies, married to the more powerful medieval barons, were always surrounded by a number of attendants who fetched and carried for them and, strictly within the castle, ran errands or delivered messages.

Young male messengers, on the other hand, regularly ventured outside the castle walls on errands for their lords, delivering letters, documents, news, gifts and other commodities. It was risky work. Medieval roads, especially in remote rural areas, could be very dangerous for the lone traveller, even for an armed, militarily trained traveller like a messenger employed by a noble or royal household. Fighting expertise did not always save them from disaster. Around 1218, one Richard, who was on a mission for his master, William Marshal – then Regent for the 11-year-old boy king Henry III – was waylaid by highwaymen, who stole his money and his clothes and killed him. In 1250, Walter Clifford, one of the powerful barons of the Welsh Marches, forced a messenger on an errand for the same King Henry to eat the royal letters, complete with wax seals, which he was supposed to deliver to him. For this grave, if ingenious, insult, Clifford was stripped of his fortune. He was lucky not to be put to death or deprived of his lands, the normal punishments for the worst of all crimes in feudal England: defying his liege lord and king who by divine right was God's choice to rule over him.

CHAPTER 8

The Garrison

The medieval castle as home was always subordinate to the castle as fortress. The time had not yet arrived when royal and noble families felt safe living in unfortified houses in the open countryside, without guards, weapons, defences and all the other manifestations of armed self-defence. War was not as incessant in the Middle Ages as some historians have implied, but the risk of war or attack was always present, and whenever fighting broke out castles were always the focus of the conflict. It was, therefore, inevitable that a military presence should shadow the lives of noble families wherever they went and whatever they did.

The importance of the military was underlined by the high ranking of the constable, or castellan, who was in charge of castle security. The most senior constables were often great officers of state, commanding armies or major garrisons. Where necessary, they stood in for the king in his absence. Even the constable of a modest castle was a man of great experience in the art of war and the command of men. He was responsible for every detail of the castle defences from the state of the garrison's weaponry and ammunition to the soundness of the castle structure, the security of the castle gates and entrances, even the depth of the water in the moat.

Although maximum preparedness was the watchword for the constable and the men he commanded, the garrison was not always fully staffed. Keeping a permanent force on hand was a very expensive business, and was usually considered necessary only where a castle guarded a strategic area needing round-the-clock surveillance, or where an emergency arose in the locality. More often, the garrison was 'on call' and was summoned to perform their feudal duties only when required. This included vassals who worked on the farms or foundries on the estate and owed military as well as other services to their lord.

Whatever its actual size at any time, the garrison of a castle covered a wide range of expertise. The knights who had entered the service of their lord and were doing their 'castle guard' had been carefully trained in combat and the use of weapons. They were motivated by a sense of duty and loyalty, together with ideals of chivalry that were peculiar to their class. It was, for example, considered dishonourable to attack an unarmed opponent. Not all knights observed such rules of *noblesse oblige* and behaved honourably at all times, but a large number did.

Several knights in a given garrison would have been based at a castle for a number of years, having entered the lord's service as young pages or squires. They were therefore familiar with the fine detail of the castle defences, its rooms, staircases and passageways as well as the surrounding countryside and its potential for both defence and attack.

The knights were the most prestigious of the men-at-arms in a garrison, but they received few privileges. There was provision for them to stable their horses in the castle bailey, which formed the outer wall of the castle, where the animals were tended by the stable marshal and his farriers. But in early medieval times no special quarters were set aside for the knights themselves; instead, they had to bed down at night with the castle servants in towers or basements or wherever else there was room. Some managed to find places in the great hall of the castle. Others, though, had to resort to lean-to shelters against the walls. Knights on castle guard duty slept at their posts.

Later, when larger garrisons were installed in some castles, better provision was made to cope with the increased numbers. Another motive for improved conditions was the fact that these later garrisons were often made up of mercenaries, who were, presumably, not as strongly attracted as the knights, if at all, by calls to duty and fidelity. Instead, they had to be tempted to their task by more luxurious arrangements. Consequently, special barracks were constructed to house mercenary garrisons in later medieval times. Mess halls were provided for leisure use and special kitchens were added to the castle's facilities.

Castle warfare was primarily siege warfare, since siege engines could be vital to defence as well as important in attack. A castle's carpenters, engineers and smiths of various skills were needed to make sure that, when required, the mangonels, trebuchets, ballistas and other engines of war were fit to fling missiles over the castle walls to cause death and destruction in the ranks of a besieging army. The range of these engines was impressive. A trebuchet, for instance, could hurl a missile weighing 136kg over a distance of 457 metres. Until the fourteenth century, when the increasing use of gunpowder enabled castle walls to be blown up and demolished, siege engines were the most dreaded weapons on medieval battlefields.

The most feared hand-held weapon at the disposal of castle garrisons was undoubtedly the crossbow, which could be loaded with its bolt, or quarrel, in advance of an attack and fired immediately danger loomed. This vicious weapon, a favourite of snipers and assassins, could penetrate a knight's plate armour at a distance of 182 metres. It was so destructive that it was banned by the Church in 1139. This, needless to say, did not prevent its continued use. Swords, battleaxes, lances, maces, arrows fired through slits in the castle walls, and even hammers with spikes were other regular weapons of medieval warfare, but a castle siege did not always come to hand-to-hand fighting. Instead, a garrison might prefer to wait for their advantages to work in their favour.

Although a garrison under siege was sealed in with no easy escape through the surrounding enemy lines, they could make preparations to ensure that they were in a better position than the besieging force. It was possible, for instance, for a garrison of only sixty men to fend off an army ten times that number by means not easily available to their foes. For a start, castle walls were immensely thick, measuring between 2 and 4 metres or more, particularly near the ground where castle builders strengthened them to withstand assault by battering rams.

Sitting out a siege meant careful preparation. Sufficient food and water were vital. Some castles, built near rivers or streams, had posterns or water-gates, but under siege conditions these might be damaged or destroyed by the enemy. It was much safer to dig wells deep inside the castle walls, where attackers could not get at them and cut off the water supply. Extra horses were brought in, complete with harnesses. Livestock were also assembled within the castle walls to provide fresh meat. The numbers could be considerable. In Lancaster castle in 1215, for instance, 80 cows and 130 sheep were quartered in the bailey. Ample stocks of bacon, ham, herring and other fish were salted and preserved. Scores of barrels were filled to the brim with grains and beans. Supplies of wine and malt and barley for making beer were also stockpiled. Corn was brought into the castle in bulk, to be ground by hand when required. Cheese, bread, rice, figs, raisins and even eels were stored in quantity.

Weaponry and other war supplies were also augmented in case a castle was besieged. Hauberks, suits of mail armour, cords, cables, bolts, iron, lead, coal and crossbows were brought into the castle and stored, like most of the other supplies, in the basement of the castle keep. Many of the foods and weaponry were susceptible to pilfering, so precautions were taken. The storage basements often had only one door, which was of course kept locked, and only one man, the watchman, had the keys.

CHAPTER 9

The Health of the Castle

A well-populated castle containing perhaps one or two hundred men, women and children, all living in close proximity, might appear to be a health risk in an age when medical practices could be crude, medical knowledge was limited or obscured by superstition and there was little or no scientific understanding of the causes of illness, let alone its cure. The picture, however, was not quite as grim as this suggests. A castle's population had better chances of remaining healthy than people crowded into insanitary towns with inadequate drainage and no realistic defence against the spread of fearsome epidemics such as the Black Death, which killed between one-third and one-quarter of Europe's population in the 1350s. The isolation of castles, as with monasteries and nunneries, gave them a measure of quarantine and, in addition, regular precautions were taken in castles to ensure some level of hygiene.

Water was provided on each floor, either at a drawing point from a well, or by means of a reservoir or cistern sited on an upper level: pipes carried the water down to the floors below. There were also facilities for hand-washing in a 'laver' or basin built into recesses, and a waste pipe made of lead carried the water away once it had been used.

Latrines, euphemistically known as garderobes, were built, where possible, into the thickness of the castle wall; if the wall was not thick enough, a projection, or corbel, was built to jut out from the wall and support the garderobe, which stood directly above the castle moat, or a river if there was one. Long shafts reaching almost to the ground were another method of getting rid of the waste and the hay that was used as toilet paper. Some castles had several garderobes grouped in a tower pattern, with a pit provided below. Sometimes kitchen drainage was used to flush waste down the garderobe shaft.

Dangers remained, though, whatever precautions were taken. People at work in the castle, from cooks to carpenters, could cut themselves and find the wound become infected. A fall could produce similar injuries, with similar consequences. Conditions such as appendicitis, diarrhoea or various fevers, which are easily cured today, could just as easily kill in medieval times.

Calling in a physician to tend a sick or injured patient was something of a lottery. There was no unified medical training, and no single school of thought as to which treatments were suitable for which conditions. The physician who arrived at a castle or other residence might rely on astrology for the purpose, or could specialise in divination, or look to the influence of the stars, the patient's destiny, the degree of sin of which he was guilty – all, or any, of these might play their part in diagnosis and treatment.

Many people, but particularly the peasantry and the poor, placed most faith in folk medicine, the ancient wisdom handed down from one generation to the next and which, in medieval times, was practised mainly by women. Magic, secrecy and ritual played a prominent part in folk medicine and exercised great appeal in an innately superstitious age. Healing herbs, for example, if picked when facing south at sunrise, were thought to have extra potency, which increased even further if charms were chanted while the picking was in progress. Similarly, St John's Wort was believed to cure fever, but only if found by accident, preferably on Midsummer's Eve.

There was not as much hocus-pocus in all this as might be imagined. Some herbs and plants certainly possessed curative properties and a number of drugs used in modern medicine are based on these prop-erties. Serious illnesses, epidemics and pandemics were clearly beyond the scope of folk medicine, but there were, nevertheless, rituals that were thought to be beneficial. Protection against the plague, it was supposed, could be achieved by a mixture of mustard and garlic. Freshly cooked, still-warm bread pressed against the lips, it was imagined, had the same beneficial effect. Hanging a bag of buttercups around the neck was thought to cure insanity. Fever could be cured, it was believed, by wrapping a spider in a raisin and swallowing it.

The more scientifically minded doctors – scientific, that is, in pre-modern terms – derived their knowledge and skills from ancient Greek and Roman texts, and in particular from the writings of Galen, a Greek physician and anatomist who lived in the second century AD. Galen's ideas dominated European medicine for more than 1,750 years. He was accepted without question as the authority in medical matters and his voluminous writings as the medical 'bible' to follow. Galen was no quack. For example, he discovered that the veins and arteries were filled with blood, not air, as had previously been believed, and he was the first to use the pulse as a diagnostic tool.

But unquestioning acceptance of Galen's ideas had severe drawbacks and resulted in the totally erroneous theory of the four bodily 'humours' that dominated medical practice until well into the nineteenth century. Galen was not the originator of this theory, which was postulated as early as 400 BC, long before he was born. The human body, it was suggested – and widely believed – contained four different types of bodily fluids, or humours. Over the centuries, the humours varied, but Galen's own choice of sanguine (blood), melancholic (black bile), choleric (yellow bile) and phlegmatic (phlegm) became the best known. According to Galen, his four humours needed to be in balance if good health was to be achieved.

Ensuring this balance could involve some drastic procedures. One was bloodletting or phlebotomy, the most ancient of all medical treatments and the most widespread. It was performed by barber–surgeons rather than the physicians themselves, and was used to reduce the excess of 'hot' fluid thought to be present in fevers and inflammations. Bloodletting proved in many cases to be a high risk strategy, killing rather than curing the patient. Even so, it had its benefits in the treatment of heart attacks, hypertension and other conditions in which blood pressure became unacceptably high.

Cupping was another treatment that lasted many centuries beyond medieval times. In cupping, glass cups were applied to the skin to draw the blood to, and even through, the surface. Cupping was used for disorders associated with too much blood in the system and, like bloodletting, was seen as a means of reducing the pressure exerted by the excess fluid.

Medicine was not left entirely to the physicians nor to the folk healers. The Christian Church strongly suspected that medicine and its practitioners were akin to those sinister magicians of pre-Christian Britain, the Druids. Folk medicine in particular smacked of pagan superstition and was said to derive from the practices such as the casting of spells, incantations, witchcraft, black magic and other heathen rituals.

This could not be acceptable to a Church that fought hard throughout the Middle Ages to destroy the heathen faiths of Europe. But churchmen also had their own religious reasons for remaining suspicious of scientific medicine, such as it was in their time. For one thing, the study of anatomy was frowned on because it involved dissecting bodies. Since Man had been made in the image of God, critics argued, cutting up the bodies of human beings was the same as cutting up God, and for this reason the practice was outlawed.

Another faith-based view of sickness, encouraged by the Church, was that disease and injury were not physical problems, but punishment from God for wickedness and sin. Medieval Christians were innately fearful of the wrath of God so that the idea of divine retribution was not difficult to accept; nor was penance and pilgrimage to holy shrines as the means of obtaining forgiveness. Besides this, the old super-stitions of good and bad luck, the Evil Eye, the Devil and all his works and the presence of demons and spirits in everyday life were still powerful beliefs that exerted a pervasive influence on the medieval mindset.

THE HEALTH OF THE CASTLE

It was inevitable, then, that even in a small, isolated castle community, many different concepts of medicine – scientific or traditional, practised by physicians or folk healers – should be in play. Which type of treatment won out over the rest when illness or accident struck a member of the community depended on how much faith the patient placed in the practitioner who came to the castle gates, and what he or she was able to do to find a cure.

CHAPTER 10

Jousting, Hunting and Hawking

In the Middle Ages, jousting, hunting and hawking were the major sports for lords, knights and other members of the upper class. Of these sports, jousting at tournaments was the most dramatic and the most dangerous. Tournaments made heroes of knights who spent a large part of their time moving from one event to the next, gathering plaudits for their prowess, the adoration of innumerable ladies and of young boys who longed to emulate them, and, often, a great deal of money in the process.

It was not surprising that the tournament held such attractions. It provided a glamorous public spectacle, featuring splendidly caparisoned horses,

colourful heraldry, knights clad head to toe in gleam-
ing armour, arrays of flags and pennants and, finally,
the thunder of horses' hooves as the knights rode
towards each other at speed, culminating in the clash
of lance upon lance.

Tourneys, as jousting at tournaments was known,
were used as a rehearsal for war and though ostensibly
friendly the dangers were sometimes no different from
the real thing. Death or serious injury were frequent
risks, so much so that in 1139 Pope Innocent II issued
an edict banning tourneys. It made no difference. The
Pope was ignored and the tournaments continued. So
did the mishaps. Even royal princes were not immune:
Geoffrey, Duke of Brittany, the fourth son of King
Henry II, fell from his horse and was trampled to death
at a tournament in 1186. At a tournament at Chalons
in France in 1274, tempers frayed and spilled over into
such violence that seventy knights were killed in what
became known as the Little Battle of Chalons. The
English king, Edward I, narrowly escaped becoming
one of the casualties.

The thrill of the tournament for the young knights who took part was its action and excitement – and the break it offered from the routine and often uneventful round of 'castle guard', which was part of the feudal duty they owed to their lord. Riding out into the tiltyard armed and armoured for battle at or soon after dawn provided an exciting prospect. The tourneys could last all day and would finish only when daylight ran out at dusk.

In the thirteenth century, tournaments featuring large numbers of 'opponents' began to give way to single combat. Safety precautions were introduced. The sharp points of lances and swords were changed to blunted ends and the tournament became a piece of entertainment. Prizes were awarded to the most daring knights, often by the same women who judged their performances. Chivalry, the medieval rite of honourable behaviour, also found a place at tournaments, as did the rules of courtly love. It was permissible for a knight to become champion to a married lady, and to beg from her a token such as a ribbon, a scarf, a veil and even a detachable sleeve from her gown. A knight would display these favours on his arm or the front of his helmet or tie them to his lance. Once the tourney was over, he dedicated his performance to his lady.

Hunting was a particular favourite of the Norman kings of England, and large tracts of woodland were specially set aside for this activity. The royal forests were forbidden territory for local people who had once been accustomed to use them to gather firewood or hunt small animals. Severe punishments were imposed on anyone who contravened the laws of the forest, where only the king and those with royal permission were allowed to hunt the fallow deer, roe and wild boar that roamed the woodland.

The hunt was less public than the tournament, but it was also more bloodthirsty and less of an exhibition of noble prowess. For one thing, the hunt was carefully prepared in advance to ensure a successful outcome. The huntsman was a professional, specially employed to stalk the chosen quarry – a deer, hart or wild boar – while the hunting dogs, tightly leashed, were brought along by their handlers. It was the dogs who found the quarry's spoor and the huntsman who took it from there to find other useful evidence.

The huntsman examined the bushes and other vegetation round about, estimating a deer's size and age from the height of the velvet its antlers had left on the trees. He also measured the height of the scratches made by the deer's horns on nearby bushes. If the huntsman suspected that the prey was close by, he would climb a convenient tree in the hope of catching sight of it. This would also give him an idea of the direction the prey was taking through the forest.

In order to intercept the prey, the dogs were taken by a roundabout route to the right spot, so that their scent would not provide a premature alert to their presence. These dogs needed careful handling, for they were truly vicious. One particularly fierce type was a bloodhound called a lymer, which had to be kept on a leash from the moment a quarry was at bay until the time arrived to finish it off.

Two lymers were taken in first, by huntsmen advancing on foot. Their purpose was to drive the prey towards the hunting party. The lord then sounded a series of notes on his olifant, or hunting horn, as a signal to the greyhounds to set about the prey and kill it. A quarry's chances of escape were not high, but if a chase ensued, it continued until the hounds had it at bay. One of the hunters was chosen to kill the animal with a single thrust of his lance. Or, sometimes, the hunting party dispatched it with bows and arrows. Afterwards, the prey was skinned, divided up, including a share for the dogs, and laid out on its skin.

Deer were a summer prey for the huntsman, since that was the time when they were at their fattest. They were by no means easy to hunt and kill, but they were completely outclassed by the wild boar, which was hunted in winter and possessed formidable weapons in its strong, curved tusks. The boar also appeared to be more intelligent, and often refused to be flushed out from cover, no matter how much the lord blew his horn or the hunting party shouted and roared.

A dog specially trained for hunting wild boar, the aulant, was employed. This was a very powerful animal, and had to be, for when a boar finally emerged from its den, it came out spoiling for a fight and had the sharp tusks to make good the threat it represented. A wild boar could, in fact, slit a man from knee up to breast in one stroke.

A successful day's hunting was much more than a chance for some sport in the countryside or an opportunity to escape the stone-bound confines of the castle for a day. The animals killed provided extra meat for the castle menu, while hawking or falconry afforded some choice game and fowl. Falconry had a special attraction as a sport, for it was the only form of hunting that could reach high into the sky and bring down its prey from beyond the range of arrows. Female falcons were preferred to males, because of their larger size and more aggressive nature. The favour shown to a pet falcon may appear extra-ordinary, but there were good reasons for the bird to be allowed into its owner's bedroom and to spend most of the day in his company, either perched on the back of his chair or carried on his wrist. The relationship between falcon and owner had to be a close and constant one, since the sport involved ordering the bird into action to carry out the owner's commands to the letter. Training a bird to achieve that standard took much time and patience.

Falcons were caught at a very young age, often before they had left the nest. The falconer, who was in charge of training the bird, started by sewing her eyelids together. This was only temporary, and was backed up by a hood placed over the bird's head. The purpose was to enable training to concentrate on developing the bird's sense of touch, hearing and taste. The falcon became accustomed to being carried about on the falconer's wrist, until he was able to remove the stitching over its eyes and reintroduce her to the daylight.

Falcons were excitable creatures, but with much patience and gentleness, the falconer trained her to sit quietly on her master's wrist both inside and out of doors and on horseback. The next step was to train the falcon to return to her master once she was let loose to hunt down her prey. This was done by means of a lure, in the form of a bird's wings tied to a piece of meat. A long cord was attached to the bird's leg to ensure she did not fly away. She was given a taste of the meat and was then taught how to spring up off the ground and seize it as it was whirled in mid-air. Finally, the fully trained falcon flew free and without restraint, ready to hunt down rabbits, hares or cranes at her master's bidding, but always returning to his wrist once her task was accomplished.

Medieval people certainly knew how to enjoy themselves, but their pleasures had limitations. Whatever they did and wherever they did it – travelling, gaming, gambling, socialising, feasting, jousting, sleeping – was controlled by the military ethos of their society. Armed escorts were imperative for journeys beyond the security of the castle. The communal nature of so much of their activity spoke of safety in numbers. Castle facilities were not designed primarily for personal comfort – though a great deal of that was provided: the real purpose was to make the castle secure against a siege by ensuring self-sufficiency within its walls and, with that, a viable, successful defence.

At the tournament, war was turned into a sport, and the most successful knights in the lists became the much-admired athletes of the day. But the real aim of jousting at the tournament was to keep knights and their horses in trim for a day that must one day come, when they faced real foes in battle, not friendly rivals. These were the realities of the dangerous world that took close on a millennium to regain the stability that was lost when the Roman Empire fell. It followed, therefore, that they were also the facts of life in a medieval castle.